tobacco blossoms,

and the pulled-tight twine

Poems by
Nancy Tripp King

MAIN STREET RAG PUBLISHING COMPANY
CHARLOTTE, NC

Cover and inside drawings by Pam King
Image page 62 by M. Scott Douglass

ISBN 1-930907-30-3

Pure Heart Press
Main Street Rag Publishing Company
4416 Shea Lane
Charlotte, NC 28227
www.MainStreetRag.com

Acknowledgments:

Piedmont Pedlar: "Carved In Stone," "The Way It Was"
Main Street Rag: "The Commandment," "Illiterate"
Anthology: "Patted Into Place," "Wood, Soap, and a Cast-Iron Pot"
GSU Review: "Through The Phone, I Hear Her Call Him Sweetie"
Licking River Review: "The Landlord"
Arnazella: "Firewood"
Pembroke: "Woman's Work," "The Old Ways"
Skylark: "Passage Into Womanhood"
Slant: "Everybody's Business"
Wellspring: "Grandeur," "Definitions," "A Different Language"
White Heron: "The Lone Journey"
The River's Edge: "Perspective," "Lifestyles And Legacies," "Yes Sir"
ProCreations: "The Color That Counts"
Timber Creek Review: "When Things Aren't Like They Seem"
Footprints: "Stains," "You Can't Wear Black Under Everything"
Pegasus: "Lessons Handed Down"
Red Owl: "Tracks"
Showboat: "Today I Wore Black," "What Everybody Knows," "Inheritance"
Bay Leaves: "Cures," "Laced Together Around The Crown"
Ginger Hill: "Once Was Enough"
Lonzie's Fried Chicken: "Almost Out Of The County"
Riverrun: "I Wish I'd Asked Mama: How Did You Feel..."
Wilmington Child: "The Power Of Two Few Words"
Ibbetson: "Worrying To Remember"
Hidden Oak: "Pinned Tight"
Fox Cry Review: "From Two Cold Stones"
Award Winning Poems: "Swing Low, Sweet Chariot," "Visions,"
"Afflictions," "When The Pressure Is Great Enough," "Gospel"

I am deeply grateful to the editors of the above publications in which
these poems first appeared, sometimes in a slightly different version,
and also to:
Dr. Steven Cohen, who said I should write, and so I wrote.
Terry McCoy, who taught me love of non-rhyming, and then taught me.
Friends, too numerous to mention, who gave me help, support, and
advice.
My critique group: those who came, went, and stayed.
The North Carolina Poetry Society for its nurturing soil.
M. Scott Douglass for his wealth of expertise and patience.
My kids, Pam and David, and daughter-in-law, Kim, who know these
stories.
Amanda, my soul-mate.
And especially to my husband, Calvin, for keeping sane amidst this
insanity.

~~~~~~~ for ~~~~~~~

Pam and David

Jackie, Lee, and Laura Ann

CONTENTS

I. THE TWIST OF THE TWINE

II. STARK AGAINST THE SKY

III. YOU CAN'T WEAR BLACK UNDER EVERYTHING

~~~~~~~ **I.** ~~~~~~~

THE TWIST OF THE TWINE

ALMOST OUT OF THE COUNTY
—for Lenard D. Moore

He tells me to always mention
my hometown.
I tell him I didn't have one:

born at the north end of Wayne County
at a signpost junction outside Saulston,
not even on the map.

We moved from there, and then twice more
before my remembrance that came further south
at the dead end of a dirt road.

When I was six, we moved across the river
and almost out of the county,
close to Jim Hines' Crossroads where northbound

one-eleven and fifty-five intersect;
where you had to go through
to get to anyplace else.

CARVED IN STONE

According to the census taken every year,
my Daddy, the oldest of thirteen,
was born in 1904
in the county of Wayne and named
Clyde Arthur.

Granddaddy and the married neighbor-lady
he was messing around with
had picked that name
for whichever one had a boy first.
Grandma suspected something was up,
so she began to call her baby *Jack*.

And Jack he was,
except when the army 4F'ed him
during the Second World War
for being too old and having a wife and two kids.
Uncle Sam hailed him as the census had.

Birth certificates weren't common
for the poor back then, so Social Security,
a respecter of age and skeletons in closets,
thumbed their noses at Uncle Sam's census.
Sent Daddy his check every month
as his mama had called him.

When his Maker called him home
he, too, called him *Jack*.
It says so right there on the stone.

THE WAY IT WAS

Mama was rugged stock and never complained.
Anyway, doctors were a luxury that had to wait.
Necessities, like fertilizer, Pepsi Colas,
and Beech Nut Chewing Tobacco, came first.

No one noticed Mama going blind,
and Mama never said.

My sister's two-year marriage ended. She moved
back home with twin girls still in diapers
and another girl just days from being born.
Now, Mama had a new job.

She didn't need to see weeds a hoe-handle distance away.
She had only to see sounds of hunger and soiled diapers,
the number of steps measuring distance from room to room,
the feel of fat-back and fried chicken when crispy done.

Midway the summer, I went back home to visit
with my newborn son and a stack
of Kodak black-and-whites showing
every funny face he'd made.

Mama looked at the pictures,
kept repeating,
These are good. Nancy, these are good.
She looked at every single one upside-down,

and I live with the guilt
that I said nothing.

THE STORY GOES

Daddy was a beer-drinking, poker-playing,
handsome son-of-a-gun who loved women
with long blond hair that he could wrap
around his hands tight
like the reins of a head-strong,
unbroken team of horses.

The story goes, after they wed
Mama soon tired of his wandering ways,
and to get even, cut
and permed her blond hair.
Wore it that way for years.
Turned a deaf ear when Daddy pleaded
to let it grow long and flowing.

The story goes, Daddy finally bargained
to give up beer and cards,
but didn't mention the women—
not about to admit to something
Mama might not know nothing about—
so Mama let her hair grow, and at night,
would uncoil and shake loose
the long golden strands
that reined Daddy home.

FROM TWO COLD STONES

Their first baby was not
newborn-red and wrinkled,
but smooth and clear with a head of hair
black as the midnight when she was born.
For the two silent days that comprised her life,
they left her nameless.
Empty arms etched BABY TRIPP
on a heart-shaped slab of cold hard marble.

Their second was born kicking and screaming,
her chubby, scowling face defying
even the thought of death.
Her father named her after an old girlfriend,
so she had his love by association.
Her nature demanded her mother's.
They both applied it like salve
to heal scarred hearts.

Their third was rawboned and scrawny.
Neither crying nor moving, she was born,
surely, to follow their first.
They remembered,
and their hearts hardened.

Another baby left nameless.

Days lingered into months
and Granddaddy started pressuring,
"Name this young'un, she's gonna live."
Mama and Daddy had stifled what it took
to pick a baby's name, so Granddaddy
began calling me like he'd called his firstborn
who was killed by lightning when she was five.
An old neighbor-lady chanced by and tacked on
her dead granny's middle name.

A TRAGEDY IN MOTION

"Somebody's gonna have a wreck down there one day,
driving like a bat-out-of-Hell," Daddy would say
about the dirt road we lived on,
the curve just down past our house,
the ditches deep where the state people
graded them out twice a year,
the ditch-banks dense with poke-salad bushes
head high and hung heavy with berries.

One Sunday after dinner,
Mama washing dishes and Daddy napping,
me and Rosa woke up ol' Blackie
and we snuck down there.

We gathered our dress-tails into sacks
and started picking.
We picked and toated and dumped
until we had a mountain of them berries
in the middle of that dirt road.

They lay there doing nothing,
sorry as a no-count yard-dog,
so we jumped in and started stomping.
That juice squished around
and over and under and between our toes.
That dirt got blood red.

We ran home yelling,
"Sunt'en bad's happened; sunt'en bad's happened!"
We were stumbling, pretending
we were bad off, spit
running down our chin
like a mad dog we'd seen once
running down that road.

LESSONS HANDED DOWN

We were standing at the edge of the field
in the shade of a rustling oak.
Daddy was showing Uncle James
all those missing places
where crows had pecked his corn.
I couldn't see what all the fuss was about,
so I wandered away
to the edge of their voices.

I was just a little fellow, but still,
I was old enough to know
right from wrong,
and I saw nothing wrong
with throwing those clods of dirt,
even after Daddy told me to stop,
so I threw a few more.

I really didn't see myself as David,
but with the sound of thunder,
one of those clods hit Uncle James
dead between the eyes,
and I'm here to tell you,
he didn't come crashing down like ol' Goliath.
The only thing that came down that day
was my Daddy's hand on my backside.

FROM DEPTHS I DIDN'T UNDERSTAND

It was whispered he was crazy—the husband
of our landlord when I was six—and I never told
how he'd sneak apples for us from the tree
behind the big house, and how we'd snuggle close
near the underground spring, gnawing off the red peels,
throwing them in the water, and watching them swirl
underneath the fence and onto some other man's land.

THE LANDLORD

I spent the night there once;
they were rich—
running water,
a real bathtub,
and washcloths so thick
I couldn't even wash
inside my ears.

CURES

During winter, to ward off colds, my sister and I
took enough turpentine to kill us—
two drops on a less-than-level spoonful of sugar—
always measured and administered by Daddy
when he'd take his dose.

Summers, Mama would mix us sugar and cocoa,
put it in a Sweet Society Snuff box,
give us a twig frazzled to a brush,
and we'd sit for hours on the doorstep,
two little old ladies, a'dipping and a'spitting,
a'spitting and a'dipping.

We snuck the real stuff once.
We'd never learned not to swallow.

AFFLICTIONS

For many long winters after my aunt came to visit
I thought I'd go deaf like her
and end up in some sanatorium,
visiting relatives on the weekend,
assuring them I was cured of tuberculosis,
unable to hear them in the kitchen
whispering to put my plate and glass and fork
over to the side to be scalded
when I wasn't looking.

Daddy said TB was catching,
and you'd know if you got it
'cause there'd be blood when you cough.

My aunt never again came back to visit.

And I'd see Daddy,
when he thought no one was looking,
pull out his handkerchief,
cough,
look,
put it back.

Once in a fried chicken thigh
I found blood down near the bone,
and even to this day, I'll poke deep,
searching,
afraid I'll find what I'm looking for.

FIREWOOD

Daddy chopped firewood religiously
during the slack time of winter's cold—
between pulling the last of the corn crop
and fixing the tobacco beds for gassing.

He cut piles of wood that grew
during the morning hours,
to be stacked by my sister and me after school,
into straight upright rows.

Enough wood for Mama to cook with
winter and summer,
enough to stretch the ton load of coal
he bought every fall,

and enough, our young bodies screamed,
to stoke the fires of Hell
the revival preacher had us convinced
we'd burn in.

THE ONE TIME DADDY WENT TO CHURCH

Miz Ada, the busybody, from down the road
Added me and my sister to her load
Of girls dressed properly in her car,
And she took us, oh so far,
To Seven Springs United Methodist.

In front of her, we sat in a row,
The other girls' hair sporting coordinating bows;
Ours stringing down our feed-sack backs.
Fancy attire is what we lacked
To attend Seven Springs United Methodist.

The very next Sunday we scrubbed our faces.
Soaped, even, the unseen places.
We counted cars; she'll be the next one.
We counted some more; she never did come
To take us to Seven Springs United Methodist.

Daddy said, "I'll take you there...."
He removed his hat and he walked bare-
Headed right straight to Miz Ada's pew—
He, in his overalls and his brogan shoes—
At Seven Springs United Methodist.

WHAT EVERYBODY KNOWS

My fourth grade teacher was a city slicker
but she was smart,
had us mixing math with health—
making a chart and recording,
for the week just passed,
how often we brushed our teeth and how often
we drank milk with our meals.

I knew the rule about brushing, so I flat-out lied.
Yes ma'am, brushed morning and night.
Three times Saturday and Sunday,
and on school days,
I drank the whole bottle of milk
that came with my lunch.
It was recorded.

Our teacher wrote on the blackboard:
For the next week, DAILY record your improvement.
That night, it snowed.
Five days, that snow lay on the ground.
Five days, those big yellow buses stayed parked,
and no lying, I brushed three times every day.

Back to school the teacher graded our homework.
Wrote on mine: *Where's the improvement?*
That's when I figured out
she wasn't so smart after all.
Everybody knows that poor people
who don't have a cow don't drink milk,
except at school.

DEFINITIONS
—for Shelby Stephenson

Rich meant not moving every year
between the time when Santa
clears the chimney and Daddy hangs
the next year's calendar on the wall,
the weather outside, *cold enough*, he would say,
to freeze a lizard's tail off.

Rich meant having Sunday dresses
and being the center of attention at recess,
talking about which dress you might choose
to wear on the class trip to Raleigh—
and when that day finally comes,
actually showing up in one—and it meant
having patent leather shoes with shine
still left on the toes.

Rich meant being buried
in the middle of a plowed field
in a fenced, tree-shaded cemetery
where the stones are all related
in one way or another.

WHEN THE PRESSURE IS GREAT ENOUGH

"Thing's gonna fall over one day
and somebody be sitting in there
with their drawers down,"
Mama kept fussing at Daddy
about the little house out back,
and Daddy kept telling the landlord.

But the landlord had white porcelain
and didn't see a washed away place
around back
that grew bigger every time it rained.
He didn't see the spidery darkness
me and my sister saw the one time
we dared each other and peeped in.
He never sat inside, trying to hide
behind the warped door
that closed wider and wider
the more the walls shifted.

But neither did he see,
at breakfast one rainy morning,
Mama smiling sweet at Daddy,
and Daddy figuring how *That damn toilet*
must have blown over
in that little ol' rainstorm
that sprung up around midnight—
a damp pair of overalls innocent
on a nail behind the woodstove;
still-wet brogans tucked snug underneath.

RITUAL

Daddy wore bib overalls
and a narrow-brimmed felt hat
every day of his life, but still, we could tell
when he was going someplace important.

He'd take off the hat he was wearing,
hang it on a ten-penny nail
half-sunk into a stud by the back door,
walk straight to the wardrobe
and take down from on top,
where it reigned in plain sight,
the round somber-gray box.

He'd place the box on the bed,
lift the lid off and set it aside. He'd slide
the fingers of both hands under the brim,
cupping them so as not to mess the form
he'd perfected to fit his face.
He'd brush away
an imaginary piece of lint,
bend close to the mirror and tug
to a rakish angle
this new hat that showed
no sweat-marks around the band.

A PERFECT CIRCLE

Every Saturday after breakfast
Mama would hand me the broom
of tied-together dogwood branches
and make me sweep the whole yard
as if she thought Harry S. Truman, himself,
were coming for Sunday dinner.

I'd begin at the front stoop
where underneath
Blackie dug down to cool dirt,
careful of the spreading verbena beds
as if he understood Mama
when she dared Daddy to chop them up.

I'd brush a wide, perfect circle around the bush
that bloomed white every Easter,
looking like a mountain of snow,
and at the least little gust of wind,
shaking that snow to the ground.

I'd work my way on around to the backyard;
take a break, drinking straight
from the mouth of the pump,
my hand damming the cooling flow,
and then I'd linger,
squishing my toes in the narrow, muddy trench
where the water ran off.

I'd leave until last, the side yard
and the length of chicken-wire that penned
many a meal and witnessed
many a prayer of gratitude
for not having to sweep
that side of the fence.

TRACKS

Mama finally did teach me
   to sweep the yard
      walking backwards,

to eliminate
   even my barefoot tracks
      as completely as Daddy

eliminated grass
   from the land
      someone else ruled.

WOMAN'S WORK

Too short to reach the looping-horse
I stood on an upside-down Pepsi crate,
played at filling tobacco sticks
with dog-fennel stalks,
dried corn shucks,
anything that would hang,
pretending it was tobacco;
practicing
to get the flip of my wrist right,
the twist of the twine tight,
and when it was full,
poking that stick straight up,
balancing it steady and praying
it wouldn't slide.

Summer, Daddy put me looping sand-lugs.
Bought me a tin box of Band-Aids
to pad my fingers,
the bend of my hand,
any place the wrapped-around-twine might rub,
and I was careful,
until pushed by the handers
flapping their bundles, fast and steady,
and if theirs wasn't soon taken,
shaken
as only women who've been there can do.

The pulled-tight twine
edged under the wrinkling tape,
finally pulling one end loose,
and without breaking rhythm,
I'd flick my hand,
shake free what was left clinging,
tie off the stick I'd filled,
and while stooping for another,
sneak a glance at my hand,
at the blisters swelling hard and tender,
until they ripped and bled.

PASSAGE INTO WOMANHOOD

I later learned the reason my sister wouldn't play.
Almost three years older, she was privy
to those five to seven days of slack
that I hadn't reached yet,
that I knew nothing of,

and I kept picking at her to play.

Rigid, like one condemned,
she sat in a slatted kitchen chair
just inside the door and near the woodstove,
close to the warmth where Mama was cooking,

and I kept picking at her to play.

I suppose I was told to stop—
by her, by Mama—I don't remember.
I only remember Mama speaking to my sister
as one woman to another,
"If you'll slap her, she'll leave you alone."

Pam King

~~~~~~~~ **II.** ~~~~~~~~

STARK AGAINST THE SKY

ILLITERATE

Daddy labored,
with his second grade education,
to form every letter perfectly—
to dot every "i" with a pressed black spot,
to cross every "t" straight and true—
as much to understand
as to be understood.

I wish I'd known enough to tell him
that even the educated,
in their struggle against time,
will often make everything handwritten
unintelligible.

THE COLOR THAT COUNTS

The family who lived down the road a piece
was black, and like us, trying to survive
on two-thirds of four acres of tobacco.
We'd swap work; Monday at their place,
Thursday at ours.

We'd start at sunrise, and when that black gum
started sticking, matting arm hairs and dragging
across apron fronts and bib overalls,
and when the morning dew and sweat mingled,
streaking the black dirt
that settled into and onto everything,
you didn't think about color.

At ten o'clock, when somebody'd go to the store
for Pepsis and Square Nabs
and those cream-filled Moon Pies,
and we'd take a break, worn slap out,
the grownups sitting on the emptied tobacco truck,
teenagers out of sight in the barn door
around on the other side, and young'uns
sprawled on piled-up tobacco sticks,
you didn't think about color.

At days end, energy gone,
and God pushing dark
faster than you could hustle
those loaded sticks into the barn,
to be poked by muscled arms
to the limbered studs straddling the tier poles,
you didn't think about color.

The only color that counted
was the ripe color of leaves cropped;
the color that would cure to a gleaming gold
and lay proud in a flat basket at the auctioneer's feet
on some warehouse floor.

HER NAME WAS JANE

She knew tobacco;
first as a hander—too short and standing
on the low stool her Daddy made
(then forced her to use),
those few inches making her
plenty big to handle the job.

Still too young,
arms too short, she became a looper,
and when she'd flip the bundles
of green tobacco across the stick,
the leaves would drag across her breast
like one of her brothers at night
copping a feel.

She knew trucking,
and would volunteer when there was a need,
knowing never to go down a wrong row,
and could handle a cropper
with the finesse of a madam
making her biting cuss-words
feel like caresses, and it was
told that when the last man finished,
still she'd ask, *Who's next?*

After we graduated, she moved close
to a cigarette factory in Richmond,
and her name was Jane.

"YES SIR"

As if it were yesterday
I can still hear my Daddy saying,
"Yes sir, the sorriest, no-count woman
is better than the best man,
and you should honor women."

I can see Mama and Daddy
come in from the fields
to eat the noon meal she'd cooked
before he ever saw the light of day.

I can see her rush through the dishes,
making time to wash out a few pieces
and get them on the clothesline
before Daddy woke from his nap,
and they went back to the fields.

"Yes sir...."

A DAY OF REST

Sunday dinner of fried chicken
fresh-killed off the yard;
butter-beans, black-eyed peas, and okra
straight from the garden;
new-scratched potatoes boiled whole
with the skin, pink and scrubbed clean
like kids sent off to church;
cornbread, oven-crispy and piled high
on the cracked, yellow-flowered plate;
dumplings smothered in a boiled sugary-syrup,
the apples picked damp with morning dew;
and that evening,
Mama taking a nap.

THREE SQUARES A DAY

Even breakfast was one of the three squares,
not a mug of spiced tea and a sliced Macintosh
as sits before me now. And more has changed.
I no longer salt each slice from habit.

Mama poured salt into her hand, a measure
to add to the pot while cooking, and Daddy
reached for the shaker to salt cantaloupe,
tomatoes, fresh sliced cucumbers
straight from the garden to the table,
and also, to salt apples
that never were, nor part of, a meal.

Unless you count jelly—
red peelings and sugar boiled down,
strained clear as sin,
sealed in jars, and stacked away
on shelves in the pantry
to wait for the noon-times when Mama
would hurry in from the fields
to fry up some ham
and make some biscuits for a meal
that was a little less than square.

WHEN THINGS AREN'T LIKE THEY SEEM

Mama watched Oral Roberts every Sunday morning.
To justify sitting for that thirty minutes,
she'd shell peas or beans for that day's dinner,
her fingers flying
as if they contained her failing sight.

We never watched TV during daylight, except then.
Daddy would fuss that it was all fake,
but he'd sit there,
not helping Mama shell a single pod,
just looking ill as hell.

When emotions rose, he'd grunt
and spit Red Man
into the tin can that sat beside his chair,
the plop seeming to echo his sentiments
on the subject of put-on religion.

The camera would pan close,
and Oral Roberts would plead
for the infirm to walk the aisle to the altar
and for the homebound to place their right hand
on the television set, or over their heart.

Mama's fingers stayed focused,
and the devil himself
couldn't have moved Daddy from his chair,
and every Sunday at that exact moment he'd declare,
"This ain't nothing but hogwash."

That statement made,
he'd lay his hat on the floor,
lean his head back against his chair,
close his eyes and lace his fingers together
way up over the left side of his chest.

STAINS

We knew we weren't angels, but even Mama
wasn't exempt from the way Daddy would grunt
and snarl his mouth in anger.

He'd pet his pigs, but not us.

What we got was an open hand drawn back,
a teasing that never found its mark
but left its mark,

driving us tighter within ourselves,

the way he'd drive the hogs
into a corner on a bone-chilling,
hog-killing day.

The moment would pass and for him, gone,

but the stain remained on us
like bacon grease splattered on an unpainted
kitchen wall, and it wouldn't wash off,

no matter the amount of scrubbing.

PATTED INTO PLACE

I only saw Mama dance once;
it was at a barbecue dinner.
Daddy had one every year for the hands
after the tobacco was housed.
We'd all eaten with a hunger bigger than our bellies,
and in the front yard's oak shade,
the grownups rested
in cane-bottomed chairs tilted back,
the legs poking holes into the solid earth.

Inside, away from disapproving eyes,
us girls giggled and flirted and bopped
to the music of a cropper's guitar.
He was older than us and, by rights,
belonged outside, but his soul was young,
and he played a mean rock-a-billy—
sounded almost like Elvis—and we pretended
that he was the king.

Finished in the kitchen, Mama came through,
headed outside. Almost to the door she turned,
and speaking as if only to herself, said,
I can dance.
She bounced in place
for a second to get the rhythm,
then cotton-eyed-joe'd to the linoleum's center
where the color was worn thin,
black creeping up from beneath.

She danced as if too young to see,
her blond hair finally escaping
its tightly pinned bun.

She danced to the door,
glanced through the screen and stopped still
as if her feet no longer could feel the beat.
She patted her hair
back into place as best she could
and walked straight outside.

WOOD, SOAP, AND A CAST-IRON POT

Summer, as well as winter,
walls of split wood stood—
short, straight, and stacked
waist-high to dry
between lanky pines and propped-up stakes—
each piece innately judged and cut
to fit Mama's stove.

Winter, Mama made lye soap *that could*, she said,
take the skin right off your hands, and year round,
when she could make a slack day,
she'd start a fire under the wash-pot,
raking wood-chips close to its three stubby feet,
and when the flames started licking
the round, smutty bottom,
she'd pile on all the charred chunks of wood
she'd doused and left scattered to dry
from the last time.

The water would dance before simmering
and she'd ease in
a half-block of that cured, cream-colored,
innocent-looking soap. Her face flushed,
she'd grip the long-handled wooden paddle
and keep the clothes poked down under the steam
until all the grease, tobacco gum, and ground-in dirt
had been eaten out.

PINNED TIGHT

Wash hung on the line,
forecasting the weather
like the six a.m. news:

Dead still and drooping
like tobacco
parched on the stalk.

Swaying lazily like a field
of golden wheat caressed
by a breath of breeze.

Popping and snapping
like a harvest-ready corn crop
in a calloused, unforgiving wind,

and always,
Mama's wash pinned tight
for whatever might come.

EVERYBODY'S BUSINESS

Daddy came home from the store,
flung a pack of Winstons on the kitchen table,
said if we were going to smoke,
not to slip around.

I quit, failing at inhaling anyway,
but Rosa kept on, and Daddy began to add
a pack of Winstons to the bag
every third day at Hoss Pierce's Store
where he went daily
for Sweet Society and Beech Nut,
charging when our money ran out
and paying up during tobacco selling season.

Rosa was up to a pack a day
and would hoard her lunch money to buy
on days when Daddy didn't.
If she was short, I'd help her
rob the hens' nests for enough eggs
to trade for the difference,
me pinning their pecking heads back with the stick
that propped open the hen house door,
and fast as the flash of a match,
Rosa's hand was under and out.

Like thieves, we'd sneak those stolen eggs
to that new store across the road
where Daddy never went because he didn't want
all his neighbors knowing his business.

WHEN ONLY BLOWS WERE ABUSE

Daddy never hit Mama,
and when he'd bring news from the store to the table
about some husband who had beaten his wife,
Mama would say, *He might beat me once*
but he'd have to sleep sometime,
her threat as predictable
as the fluffy, crusty biscuits she made
for most every meal.

If time was tight,
or the wood, damp and slow in burning,
she'd make flour-bread,
the dough patted flat in her hands and cooked
on top of the stove over the opened eye
in a cast-iron frying pan heavy enough
to bust a hole in a man's head.

I've inherited that seasoned pan, and I wonder
if she could have used it in the dead of night
if she'd ever had the need—but she never did—
she never suffered abuse.
She only suffered
his long bouts of angry silence.

INHERITANCE

Daddy never owned a spade of dirt
except the plot that held his tombstone,
and that only after he died,
but he was fond of saying, "My Daddy left me
this whole wide world to make a living in."

Every Sunday after dinner, he'd leave us
still sitting at the table and he'd go straight outside,
turn his truck so it faced the road,
tip his hat low on his forehead, and then,
just sit inside. The sun, beating down
through the rolled-up windows,
was a comfort to his silence.

All afternoon he'd sit there,
one hand draped over the steering wheel
as if he were some wealthy aristocrat,
eyes narrowed, watching
his world go by.

PERSPECTIVE

Billowing smoke delayed the rising sun
as flames snaked from underneath
the rusted tin roof of our tobacco barn
full of the third cropping:

> Leaves the width of two hand-spans.
> Promises the color of gold.
> Stems not quite dry.

Strangers were drawn from the highway
like moths, and neighbors converged
to share the helplessness of watching
dreams become ashes.

In the crackling silence, a powerful kinship ignited
and emotions hung heavy as the haze of fog
until Daddy said, "Well boys,
that's one way to kill it out, ain't it?"

THE COMMANDMENT

I'd heard Daddy, many times, tell Mama
he'd give his right arm if he could get his hands
on the page of recorded births in the Family Bible
passed down to his Aunt Pat—
one name written,
and him called something different all his life—
his given name not dying with his parents,
but living on in snickers down tobacco rows
of how to make him fighting mad.

At sixteen, romancing my way toward marriage
and premature motherhood,
I searched family names in that Bible,
mating and tasting their sound upon my tongue.

There was that fated page,
the flourishing pen-strokes like the serpent,
twisted and laying wait in the Garden,
and God forgive, I lay my hand flat
on that factual page like a preacher
making a point during a sermon.

I pressed, tugging sideways, until it gave up
its hold on the Bible's thread binding.
I pressed, until separated, it lay loose
    —a thing apart—
and when no one was looking,
I gathered that fragile page into a fist-tight ball.
I stuffed it down my scooped neck dress
and snuck it home to Daddy.

I pointed to the name he never recognized.
He stared an eternity,
his face like stone,
his hands trembling.

My delirium fell slowly from my body
the way rotting flesh must surely
fall from bones. Then, with a look
I could not read but will never forget,
he turned without speaking and walked
with the shuffling gait of a condemned man
into the kitchen where Mama was cooking.

With his bare hand on the handle,
he lifted the woodstove's lid,
dropped that crumpled page inside,
and we all three just stood and watched
those flames lick and shrivel as if they were
the fires of Hell.

REDEMPTION
—for Aunt Flora

As driven as a salmon swimming upstream
Uncle John would pull two drunks a year—
first, when the tobacco beds were gassed
and laying wait under white plastic, and again,
when the last barn of that tobacco was cured—
those times etched in my aunt's dread
as deeply as the need instilled in him.

He'd start on store-bought liquor,
driving half-drunk across the county line
for more, and when he'd start seeing snakes
coming for him across the fields
and down the black asphalt, he'd switch
to Mason jars of rotgut,
seemingly clear as a running stream,
that some bootlegger would bring.

Uncle John drank himself screaming
into an unused back-bedroom's darkened corner,
my aunt keeping every drape in the house drawn,
pretending they weren't at home,
and in her darkened kitchen,
in sudsy scalding water,
she washed his empty jars and packed them
into boxes in the pantry,
redeeming
every last one for canning.

A LESSON WORTH REMEMBERING

Mama says there's not much difference
between a husband and dough;
that there's a certain feel when it's right
or when it needs to be worked some more.

She says biscuits, kneaded too much, won't rise,
making them weigh heavy on the tongue,
no matter how hot the oven they were in;
but that pastry is different
and must be toughened enough
to stay together
when it's dropped into a boiling pot
with an old rooster. She says
if dough's not ready you can tell
the minute you start rolling:
it will break apart,
needing
to be gathered back into a ball
and worked some more—
flattened and folded and pressed—
forcing you, when you start rolling again,
to slam the pin down hard, and then,
to keep holding that pressure.

THE GAMBLER

Again, the crops failed, but this time
the rusting Farmall Cub,
the worn-out plug mule (the only thing
that Daddy never cussed), the plows
sharpened to a ready point,
even the tobacco sticks
went to D. M. Price & Sons Fertilizer
to finish paying that debt;
and the black '57 Two-Ten repossessed
by Mooring Chevrolet for a measly
two hundred and fifty-seven dollars.

Only the '49 blue Chevy remained,
a relic from a prosperous year,
and on moving day
its three-quarter-ton bed was piled high.

We climbed into the cab,
my sister in her spot in the middle,
straddling the gearshift, and me in mine,
too heavy and too old on Mama's knee.

We waited and watched
Daddy walk out to the middle of the field
and stand
like he was Lord and Master of all.

We watched him stride back
and jerk open his door.
He stopped with one foot propped
on the running board and swore
one last time that he
could have made those sand hills pay
if it had only rained.

VISIONS

The depression was long past, but
if the landlord wanted your house
for a younger hand, it became that time again.

And you moved on.

Daddy found a place with higher hopes
and moved Mama
to a four-room excuse for a house.

Out back, standing stark against the sky,
one lone tree,
the ground beneath covered with black walnuts.

Daddy told her about the tree, but said nothing
about the house and the no-count rusted roof
that would surely leak when it rained.

He said nothing about the paint, so long peeled,
that only bits of color still clung
in the crevices sheltered under the eaves.

He didn't tell her about any of those things
that she could never put her fingers on,
and being nearly blind, she saw none of them.

She only saw the tall, fluffy cakes she'd make,
the layers piled high with a boiled egg-white icing
that was packed full of black walnuts.

EVERY TIME THE DOOR IS OPENED

My sister moved back with my parents;
went to work serving eggs
sunny-side-up before daybreak,
so the neighborhood do-gooder
hauled my three nieces
to Vacation Bible School and,
for a short time after that,
to church and Sunday School—
every Sunday—
them spit-shined and polished
as well as Mama's half-blind eyes
could make them;
the nickels Daddy doled out,
clutched in their tight and sweaty fists,
and spilling forth from their mouths
like pearls before swine,
the story of the dollars
Mama and Daddy had hidden
underneath their mattress,
and in their innocence, my nieces
multiplied those dollars like fishes;
spilled forth—every Sunday—more stories,
picked and prodded for, and they fabricated
what they thought she wanted to hear—
every Sunday—
until the welfare lady came,
cut off Mama and Daddy's check;
said someone had tipped her off
that they weren't needy.

PUT AWAY

They still heated with wood,
had an outside privy, and one spicket
in the kitchen, and it was cold—
if you wanted hot
you put the black iron kettle on to boil—
and from their pension they saved
a dollar or two each month
to bury them with, they said;
to be put away nice, and please,
not just a graveside service,
but a laying-out in a nice casket
in the funeral home's chapel,
as if they were really somebody.

WORRYING TO REMEMBER

Zen Masters say,
If you look deep into your palms
you will see your parents
and all the generations of your ancestors,
but for me and Mama, it was size.

She was once a big woman,
eyes spring-water blue
and hair like sweet-corn silk.
German, someone said at a family reunion.
She passed to me, not the coveted coloring,
but the despicable size—
the extra wide hips—
childbearing hips, old folks called them,
though she only had three children, me two,
and my daughter none.

I worry to remember at what age
Mama's flesh began to hang,
the weight-loss of time making unsightly folds
under un-elastic skin.
I worry to remember: Was it my age now?
Is this the age that my plumpness starts to droop
into my daughter's consciousness,
making her, twenty years hence,
worry to remember?

SWING LOW, SWEET CHARIOT

I sing to Mama in my tone-deaf voice,
hoping the soothing sounds
and rhythmic variations
will pull her mind
from the drowning cough of heart-failure
and quiet her restless limbs.

Talking to people that only she sees,
she's regressed to a grandmother
mad at her daughters for not getting
those young'uns outta that tree;
to a new mother suckling a baby
clutched to her breast,
and with fear quivering her voice, whispering,
If our tobacco drowns, we'll have no money;
to a young girl, fist clenched and tears streaming,
yelling at her older sister,
Stop bossing me around; you're not my mama;
to a toddler left motherless at two.

Like the time before
and the time before that,
her breathing quick and shallow,
she quiets,
curled like a little child. Now,
I've become the mother,
and I close my eyes to rest,
keeping vigil
beside this woman-child
who lingers
at a mother's voice
singing.

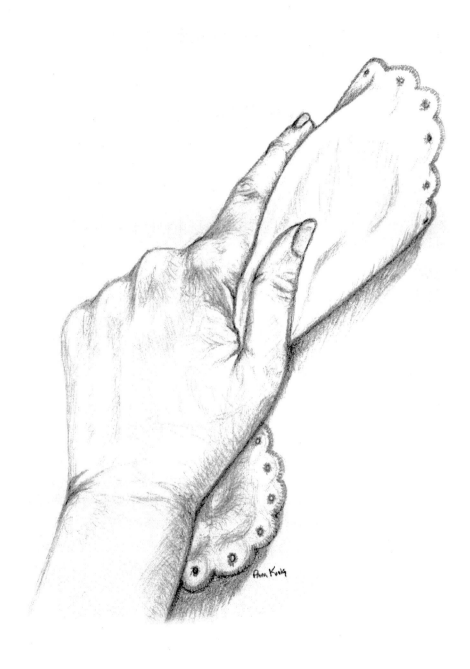

~~~~~~~ **III.** ~~~~~~~

YOU CAN'T WEAR BLACK
UNDER EVERYTHING

I WISH I'D ASKED MAMA:
HOW DID YOU FEEL...

...when your father died,
and life being for the living, you were left alone
with his corpse in the front room while Daddy
and everyone else went to the field
to barn the tobacco that refused to wait
for death's ritual?

...when you found out
Daddy had a daughter somewhere,
born before the three you bore him?
Were you glad you never had a boy
to follow in his father's footsteps,
or did you just accept it? After all,
Daddy was thirty-five when you two married,
and like you often said:
You know how men are.

...when he died, and you,
unable to see day from night by then,
forced to come live with us,
moving into our son's emptied room,
the bulk of your belongings given away
as if they were of no value?

...when alone, maybe resting
in your cane-bottomed rocker, holding
the photo of you and Daddy sitting on the steps,
his arm around your shoulders,
drawing you near to him—a gesture
Rosa and I never saw him make.

I keep that photo like I found it: on top of others
in a faded Whitman's candy box.
It, alone, was wrapped inside a paper towel
worn from much handling
as if you'd touched it often.

THE HARD LIFE

Nursing coffee over dirty dinner dishes,
my sister and I commiserated on the hard life she had
growing up. I had it easy. Even from early on,
she drew trouble like a magnet:

Too short to see the top shelf of the safe,
she'd pull up a chair to finger chunks from cakes
baked on Saturday for Sunday's dinner
where her escapades
were the usual topic of conversation.

As regular as the report cards we brought home,
her C minuses and occasional D's
received verbal tirades while my A pluses
faded into oblivion.

She was the one who skipped classes,
making Mama and Daddy pay attention
to her answers when they questioned, every day,
what we did in school.

She was the one who slipped off to meet boys,
forcing Daddy to roam the roads, searching,
only to come home and sit like some stone
Buddha until she came in.

"You were the lucky one," she said.
"You were always in a corner
with your nose stuck in a book,
and they left you alone."

I DO REMEMBER

I read somewhere,
If you can't remember your childhood
you probably were abused,
so I started trying to remember.

I recall only once getting spanked
harder than I should have been.
Rosa and I were fussing over the dishes.
Who to wash. Who to dry.
Both wanting to do neither.
Daddy stormed into the kitchen,
snatched the straw broom
propped against the safe,
and started on me since I was closer,
thrashing me like a tornado in a wheat field.

The instant he turned me loose
his mad spell fizzled,
and he never touched Rosa.
I never forgave her for that.

I do remember him calling me Little Ugly:
"Hey, Little Ugly," and "Come here, Little Ugly,"
and often he'd ask,
"How'd you get so ugly in so few years?"
And when it grew dark and he'd send me
to the woodpile or to the pump
or to close the hen-house door,
and I'd want someone to go with me, he'd sneer,
"If you weren't so mean, you wouldn't be so scared."

But for the life of me
I can't ever remember being abused.

LOVE IN A MASON JAR

Mama never gave my sister and me hugs;
it wasn't her nature—A *Dysfunctional Family*
the experts would label it nowadays—
but I remember the Christmas before Daddy died,
she gave to both my sister and me
a Mason jar filled with black walnuts.
She'd cracked
and picked them out herself
by the feel of her fingers.

THE POWER OF TOO FEW WORDS

It was at one of those family funerals,
the kind where my kids and their kids
and all these distant kin come
who you only see at times like these
and never in-between.

I overheard Uncle George talking to a chubby,
pimply-faced, stringy-haired girl
sitting off by herself.
She was the spitting image of me at that age.
He says to her, "I don't know who you are,
but if you do as good as you look
you'll be worth a million dollars."

I watched her sit taller,
straighter,
and time-faded words resurfaced:
If you do as good as you look, you'll be okay.

Those were Mama's words—
practical like the woman she was—
and I closed my eyes and mourned
the child of a Mama
of too few words.

LIFESTYLES AND LEGACIES

Basal cell carcinoma,
conjuring up visions
of bronzed bodies glistening with baby oil,
of volleyball playing tag with the water's edge,
of sandcastles and pull-tabs.
The easy life.

Plain old skin cancer:
the reality of a sharecropper's kid
pulling tobacco plants
as the sun warmed east to west,
chopping endless weeds
down endless rows that had no end,
cropping and suckering in the blazing sun
before the days of sucker control,
weed control, and harvesters.
Lucky Strikes and Big Red.

THE LONE JOURNEY

Stay and sleep with me, she murmurs,
deep into the final days
of her doctor's prediction.
I crawl in wondering
if this will be the night
she leaves us.

I hold her close
the way she held me
the winter I was eight
and she, the big sister,
whispering,
It'll be all right.

But I can't make it right
the way she did,
when through the bedroom wall,
we heard Daddy tell Mama,
*We're leaving
this worn-out land
and moving on.*

NO CHOICES

In the hospital
            corridor's
      crepe-
soled
            hushness,
      I stop
                        outside
            your closed door,
      paste a smile
against what I'll find.

"Only a tiny change,"
says the crisp voice behind the mask,
but a multitude of tiny changes
have taken their toll.

Tomorrow, again,
      there'll be that moment
            when I'll think,
                  I can't do this...
but still I'll enter.

REFUGE

I have to be willing to let you go,
but it's hard.

It's hard to know
I'll be the only one left of our family.
To be the baby, and no longer be the baby,
but the matriarch,
the monarch.

I'm scared;
I am still that child
huddled in the corner with a book,
looking for refuge in the printed word,
only now, these are my words.

And there is no refuge.

GRANDEUR
—for Rosa

Lugging a hand-planter down tobacco rows,
resetting the perished plants,
we talked of how it'd be
when we grew up—
grand ladies reclining on white satin
sheets while smoke drifts lazily from cigarettes
dangling from immaculate fingertips....
Work-weary, we'd grow silent,
the click of the metal planter
magnified in the quietness
of new-plowed earth.

Pre-teen, we traded pop bottles for Winstons.
Filter-tips. Another step toward grandeur.
You mastered the art of inhaling,
drawing smoke deep into lungs
once fresh-air and sunshine healthy.
Shamed, I admitted defeat.
You'd smoke under the cover of darkness,
the click of the cigarette lighter
magnified in the quietness
of a sleeping household.

Today you lie on frilly white satin,
peaceful after radiation and chemo,
hands folded gracefully
in the way of a great lady,
nicotine stained fingers
holding a lace hankie.
I watch as they lower
the rose embossed lid,
the click of the lock
magnified in the quietness
of the chapel.

TODAY I WORE BLACK

I've never worn black to a funeral before.
Daddy knew I hated black
so I wore a flowered dress.
Big, bright orange flowers
like the daylilies he grew.
That was long ago.
I only owned one dress.
Daddy understood.

Mama knew I hated black
so I wore a green dress.
Soft and gentle
like the lady she was.
My Sunday best, but not exactly
funeral attire.
Mama had a vain streak too.
Mama understood.

Today I wore the color of mourning,
of unbearable grief and pain.
I had a closet of colors to choose from,
but there was no choice.
You knew, Sis.
You understood.

DOWN A DIRT ROAD

At my uncle's house, me and my cousins
stand in line outside the packhouse door,
waiting our turn
and switching our dress-tails as smartly
as the mules switching flies.
A neighbor, right much older, has come to play.
He hides inside....
                    But try as I might
I can never remember
past the point of standing in line.

Out roaming back roads,
I happen upon the dirt path that leads there.
The cotton fields on either side
lay like an unblemished white blanket.
I trample the sandspur-studded ruts to the house,
the windows broken out and staring
as empty as my remembering.

The pack-house is gone,
the barbed wire fence torn down,
and not a sign of a post left standing,
only a hard hollow where the path once was—
where we waited in line—
and I walk that twisted narrow way
toward what is waiting,
toward what I can't remember,
until I am there,
the youngest of six,
taking my turn to go inside, and then,
separated by a closed door
from the voices of my cousins.

FOR DISPLAY

My crocheted sweater is not enough
against the sudden chill
as I slip past rasping corn rows
and down the path of briars and beggars' ticks
to the falling-down house where Granddaddy lived.
I need to take something back with me,
something to set on my dresser and, at will,
to touch and feel.

A piece of distorting pane.
A brick from the crumbling foundation.
Maybe even a still-green walnut from the tree
beating its loaded branches
on the tin roof of the back porch—
a conjurer of all I'd forgotten.

Too many pieces to choose from
so I leave them laying where they belong.
I turn back and look
one last time
through a gaping window,
reaching
for the fleeting warmth of a pile of coats
spread across this backroom's bed
the day after Granddaddy died—
coats my great aunt borrowed
from her circle of city friends
so we would all look respectable
at the funeral.

CRAVINGS

Deprived of a natural saltlick,
an animal will ramble his way
to the location of an artificial one.
Once there, he will stand entranced,
his rough tongue continuously caressing
the block of crystals
like a tiger bonding a newborn cub,
like our cow urging her wobbly calf,
like my calico licking the closed eyes
of her basket of babies.

My poems have become my babies.
Immediately, I want to say,
Look! Look! See this bit of newborn!
and I hold them out
for some stranger's subjective opinion.
I nurture and discipline them closer,
then hold them out again and again,
until finally, approval.

There was a block of salt in a pasture's far corner
on a farm where we once lived, and the landlord's
pair of mules had worn a path
through joint-grass and dog-fennel.
I wonder if there's a smell to salt that draws,
or if the trampled path
was only a habit they followed.
Or if there was something inside driving them
as I am driven?

ONCE WAS ENOUGH

My husband, Calvin, said he wanted no part;
left me and our son, daughter, and daughter-in-law
hovered above the Ouija Board,
our fingers clustered on the pointer.
We lightly chased the date it said
our daughter-in-law's mother would die,
but she didn't,
still hasn't,
and we never told.

The rulebook warned how unsettled spirits
will often wreak havoc, acting as imposter,
so I asked from my Daddy's spirit
facts that only I knew;
facts that I lifted my fingers from
and theirs answered correctly.

I asked how he felt about my poems
clearing his skeletons from my closets.
He said to stop, but I haven't,
still releasing secrets that no longer matter,
but still feeling guilty like I
am betraying his trust.

Like that time I parked with Calvin at the Cliffs—
deserted on a dreary December Sunday afternoon—
feeling a strange persistence pressing me,
the car windows fogging us into a warm womb,
and finally, us leaving for home
too far into the edge of dark
that Daddy had set as my curfew,
and after we had already passed the crossroads,
me telling Calvin to turn off the headlights
so Daddy wouldn't think
it was as dark as it was.

ROOM-SHARING AT THE CONFERENCE

For the second straight day I volunteered,
set my alarm,
showered and dressed first,
and now am waiting,
staring at my roommate's
same slow sounds behind the bathroom door,
only today, I am ten.... My best friend

wears a pair of shorts to school
under her dress,
lets me wear them home under mine—
a perfect tomato-red fit—
the hand-hewed pair I'd cobbled
from a blue-flowered feed-sack, bunched
under my pillow while I go and strut outside.

Lisa, the landlord's granddaughter,
comes over to play,
admires the shorts I have on and wants
only those.
We go back outside,
she in the perfect tomato-reds
and me in my crude,
cinched-at-the-waist-with-tobacco-twine,
bloused-out, faded, flowered ones.

We strut across to her grandmother's yard.
Lisa twirls like a ballerina,
telling the story of our shorts
while I stand still as a fence post,
my dress-tail pulled high to show
mine that I made.

As if touching something nasty,
Lisa's grandmother pulls at my shorts;
at the legs, un-hemmed and raveling.
She yanks at my drawstring waistband and says
my casing stitches are long enough
to snag my toes in.

Lisa snickers,
clamps both hands over her mouth,
tries to hold it in.
She gives up, throws her head back,
laughing and laughing,
leaving me with a feeling
I can't put words to...

but that I feel now,
staring at the bathroom door and knowing
my roommate's going to prance out in red,
head thrown back,
laughing.

A DIFFERENT LANGUAGE

He walks on past the slower moving poets,
leaving them lingering
over each brochured point of interest.
I lengthen my stride to reach his side—
the rain drizzling slow—and my umbrella
big enough for two and he with none.

I raise it over him and he smiles down,
the rain chill leaving,
spreading a slow warmth
like a shot of Jack Daniels
at the first feel of a chill coming on.
"Grab holt," I say,
wanting our rhythms to mesh,
my country accent jarring the air,
then settling down and around
like stirred-up dust on a dirt road.

I wait for his arm to slide around me
so I can melt into the moment
like I would when I was a young girl,
helping to top-out tobacco blossoms—
one field finished, and to move on to the next,
we all scrambling to be first
into the back of Daddy's old pickup
so we could perch on the sides,
us girls holding tight and squealing
at each mud-hole bump,
and it would work—
any boy brave enough
to elbow a seat next to a girl
would reach his arm out and around
and hold her tight
so she wouldn't fall off.

But this man,
walking bareheaded in the rain,
must not speak my language.
My offer to *Grab holt!*
quivers around forever
under that damned umbrella,
and I feel the way a water-drop must,
high-stepping on a hot skillet
before it fizzles to nothing.

The path stretches on not quite as promising.
Our steps, still not yet meshed.
The rain keeps on falling, and I say again,
this time, real inviting and soft-like
"Grab holt."

Time stops, but we keep on moving.

Then slow and easy, his hand reaches up.
Slow and easy, his fingers curl
around that damned umbrella handle.

THROUGH THE PHONE,
I HEAR HER CALL HIM SWEETIE

I want to call someone Sweetie
or maybe Babe or whatever;
to be that sure;
to use that foreign language
never spoken in our house
between Mama and Daddy,
between them and us. Once
when I did try, the words
crumpled and bunched like sheets
under a comforter on a bed
made by someone who never was taught.

Mama did teach me to make a bed,
and I want those words to feel
as natural as that;
as natural as gripping a sheet by its side,
flicking it half-straight in place, and then
billowing it high and full,
and letting it float
before settling down softly
like a whisper of love-
words through a phone,
not intended to be overheard.

YOU CAN'T WEAR BLACK
UNDER EVERYTHING

Always have done what I was supposed to,
and then I voted for Clinton.
Felt good when people said,
"No one will admit..." and I'd say, "I did."
Felt almost as good as yesterday
when I bought myself a black lace bra.
Mama never would let me buy one;
said they weren't likely to last,
you couldn't wear black under everything,
and anyway, what did I think I was,
a floozy?

LACED TOGETHER AROUND THE CROWN

I take Frost from my wall of books and close my eyes;
breathe deep his love of simple language
and embrace being raised on hard work
and the pictures in *The Grit* on Sunday.

I hold, like a love-tattered doll,
a house barren of books,
but rich in axioms quoted like a second language,
usually preceded by, *My Daddy always said...*
and I practice, still,
more than a day's work for a day's pay.

I learned God by example
and the keeping of the Sabbath
by watching Daddy watch clouds hang heavy
over hay, dry and ready to bale, and hearing him say,
"That ox ain't in the mire yet,"

and by watching him take a kitchen chair to the porch,
position the back legs in dents grooved over time,
tilt back, remove his hat, place it on his chest,
hold it with his fingers laced together
around the crown, and close his eyes.

STUDYING THE MASTERS

so much depends/upon/a red wheel/barrow/
glazed with rain/water/beside the white/chickens.
—William Carlos Williams

I never could see the connection
between a wheelbarrow and chickens,
and I knew both.

My rusted red wagon was close enough kin
to a red wheelbarrow, and every spring,
Mama raised a new flock of snowy-white hens.
The yellowed scraggly ones, too old to lay,
would become chicken & pastry
during winter's long days.
I asked Mama once, *Why winter?* and she said,
Because it's better.

Newly married and transplanted in a park
a mile past Camp Lejeune's main gate,
the temperature soaring
in our tight, tin-covered trailer,
I ignored Mama's words
and bought a pin-feathery hen from a neighbor.
I carried her home amid visions of cool salad
and a lasting pot of hot pastry.

Four boiling hours later, that hen still tough,
my bangs plastered to my forehead,
my ponytail, a sopping mop clinging to my neck,
and we go outside,
dine on deviled eggs and sweet tea.

Once, Mama broke her own rule about a hen
too old to lay and let her escape the ax—
she was a good nester and would chip a hole
in the confining calcium when a baby was ready,
and like me, ferociously pecking at a shell
too damn tough to crack.

THE SAMENESS OF THE DIFFERENCES
—for the black poet at open mike

It's taken me a long time too,
to learn that I'm of worth,
but I can't strut and shout it out like you,
knowing people will accept
from the shame of their past wrongs.

I'm shackled to the antebellum also,
but not to the grand plantation owners.
My people, back then, were crackers;
the poor illiterate white.
Trash?
Maybe. Maybe not.
Such facts aren't covered in courthouse records
or on tombstones in grown-over graveyards.

But I do know my ancestors didn't own yours,
didn't buy and sell and rape.
They were too busy scratching a living
from a too-small parcel of land, burdened
with the never-ending worry
of keeping a roof over their heads
and putting food on their table—
the same collards and fat back and sweeten taters
that you now claim only for your race.

GOSPEL

Alone in this roomful of relatives
I read my copy of our Genealogy
as if it were gospel,
keeping silent about the gossip
Great-Granny mumbled
on what she thought was her deathbed
at the end of her eighty-fifth year.
Gossip she confided as fact
after she recovered:

How her Daddy's Mama,
a shy slip of a girl in hand-me-downs twice over,
was sent to tend the ailing wife of a nearby farmer,
living there in his house through a hard winter—
tending him and his young'uns, too—
till death rattled the March windows
and the ailing wife slipped away
quietly into a peaceful night,

and how her Daddy, at that time,
was only the beginnings of a speck
of morning sickness.

She told of the farmer's hired hand,
an unmarried middle-aged man who wanted land,
and how he swapped silence
for one seeded acre and a young wife,
and the child she carried
to carry his name....

I read on down page after page of facts
that are, from then on
(as far as I know)
gospel.

THE OLD WAYS

Mama taught me how to sew;
to slip-stitch a hem with such delicate stitches
that if it weren't for the light
shining through the tail of the dress
sashaying in the afternoon sun,
you'd never know how deep that hem was.

She taught me how to make biscuits;
to work the dough knowing when to stop,
to pinch a hen-egg-sized ball
and palm-roll it perfect-round,
tucking the cut edges inside to bake
finger-printed-smooth on top.

She taught me how to hang wash on the line;
to button the long-handled underwear
so the flap wasn't gaping open,
step-ins and brassieres
behind the bed sheets
so they couldn't be seen from the highway.

She taught me how to live
with the outburst of a sharp-tongued man,
to hide the hurt until I, too,
learned to pretended
it didn't exist.

But Mama's been dead a long time now,
and in this modern age of ready-to-wear,
canned biscuits, and clothes dryers,
I've about forgotten those lessons,
and today I yelled back.

Nancy Tripp King

Like Nancy's poems tell us, she was born near Goldsboro, N.C. and reared near Seven Springs, just down the road from the Cliffs of the Neuse. At seventeen, she married a marine headed for a career in the Corps, and they moved to Jacksonville. The Kings have one son, one daughter, and one granddaughter.

Although a lover of words from early on, Nancy didn't begin writing until after her forty-eighth birthday. During these past twelve years, 154 of her poems have been published in journals such as *Slant, Mangrove, Feminist Studies, Old Red Kimono,* and *GSU Review.*

For twenty-six years, Nancy worked in Onslow County School Food Service; first at Parkwood Elementary and then at Blue Creek Elementary. She retired from the school system and became a used-car salesman in her husband's business. Three years later, they both retired again. Calvin remains retired; Nancy is as retired as a writer can be. They live with two cats, once strays, who now think they own the place, and with a dog they recently inherited.

This is Nancy Tripp King's first book.

Additional books may be obtained by sending

$15.00 plus $2.00 shipping and handling

(total: $17.00 per book)

to:

Nancy King
402 Decatur Rd.
Jacksonville, NC 28540-3757